An Introduction to Basic Elements
And Why we use them

Volume one

in the
Meat & Potatoes of
Plastic Injection Moulding
Series

Explaining WHY - makes sense

Dankerr Enterprises

An Introduction to Basic Elements
And Why we use them

This Book is aimed at the people finding themselves in and around Plastic Injection Moulding machines, which would include primarily die setters and/or technicians.

For further insights into Die setting practices and the Why's, also Troubleshooting and Die Trialling Practices including the Why's keep a lookout for these books coming soon, by **Dankerr Enterprises.**

A Basic Understanding of the environment and machinery surrounding these few elements is expected and will assist in your time in and around Plastics.

Now...This is a MUST to understand.

There are times at work when time constraints, pressure from above etc are going to take it's toll on how you conduct yourself. It is Important to understand that when taking a shortcut to ease these burdens or pressures, take care NOT to keep repeating and continually taking these shortcuts because they WILL turn into habits and (in turn) reduce you to a slap dash Die setter or troubleshooter.

Do not concern yourself about the speed of the die change &/or troubleshooting. Like everything else, the more you 'format' your approach, the smoother (& thereby the speed) of the die change and getting to the root cause of the fault will become evident.

Frequently peruse this book to rekindle the correct way to conduct yourself thereby showing your boss what you are all about.

Safe work practices that get the job done safely and efficiently shine brightly with upper management without you having to say a word.

An Introduction to Basic Elements
And Why we use them

For the Die Setter

...Achieving Optimum Die Change Times

When heading to a machine to do a die change, it is desirable that you peruse the setup sheet on the tool going in and take the desired tools with you, ancillary equipment, clamps, bolts etc. This puts everything required at the point of use thereby restricting the need to walk backwards and forwards to the die setting area or elsewhere extending the time of the die change. When the die change is complete and you walk away you will take all excess hoses ancillary equipment etc with you and put in their respective places.

This practice will not only keep everything in it's place (a home for everything right?) but it will reduce your overall die change times. You will always know where to find something, hoses ancillary equipment etc, not only this but everyone else will be able to locate the ancillary equipment, hoses etc...also will make you look like a professional which is always good in the eyes of your boss yes?

You know this is true but as I previously stated it is easy to just drop the hot runner box (or other ancillary equipment) at the nearest bench and move onto the next die change.

An Introduction to Basic Elements
And Why we use them

What this in turn does is this...yourself and others are guessing as to where this or other ancillary equipment is, which ends up with piles of stuff everywhere, am I right? How can you then professionally approach the next die change?

Don't be fooled by thinking this practice speeds up your die change times, it doesn't. It may speed up the current change but the following ones, and the following shifts die changes will be extended by this practice.

" PUT IT AWAY "

That practice and that practice alone, will speed up your die changes, keep the work place clean and thereby promoting a clean and safe environment not to mention the thoughts going through your bosses mind.

An Introduction to Basic Elements
And Why we use them

... Clamping

When clamps are being used, ideally they are positioned on the sides of the tool as opposed to top and bottom. The reason for this comes down to safety health and welfare. When using clamps top and bottom, whilst the tool is still suspended by the crane/gantry - position and bolt up the top clamps so that the tool is secured by the crane/gantry and the top clamps, then get under the machine and clamp up the bottom clamps before removing the crane/gantry and lifting strap. Now the reason everyone is slowly getting away from top and bottom clamping is firstly lying on your back trying to place and secure clamps and bolts above your face... if anything slips or falls you cop it on the chin, add to that when getting up from under the machine if you misjudge the position of cables, machine ledge or any other protrusion in the tool working area, you jar your head, back, shin or whatever else gets in the way. Obviously you try and not put yourself in this position of hurting yourself, but for these reasons side clamping is the ideal when clamps are being used. Typically, the tool room can accommodate side clamping quite easily with little expense involved.

Direct bolting is even better if your bolt holes in the back plates line up with the platen bolt holes.

An Introduction to Basic Elements
And Why we use them

The bolt should be screwed into the platens approximately **1 and ½ times the width of the bolt**. Any less and the bolt thread has an increased chance of ripping the leading threads out of the bolt hole, thus requiring being helicoiled. Any deeper than 1 ½ times the width of the bolt and you risk bottoming out the bolt and not securing the clamp.

Don't forget you are working in an environment that has material granules, grease, bits and pieces moving around, if bits get into a bolt hole, when screwing in the next bolt, it will be pushed to the base of the hole. However you can see over time this can build up and restrict the securing of the clamps by gradually filling up the hole. Just be aware of this. Typically the bolt holes go approximately 3 times the width of the bolt initially.

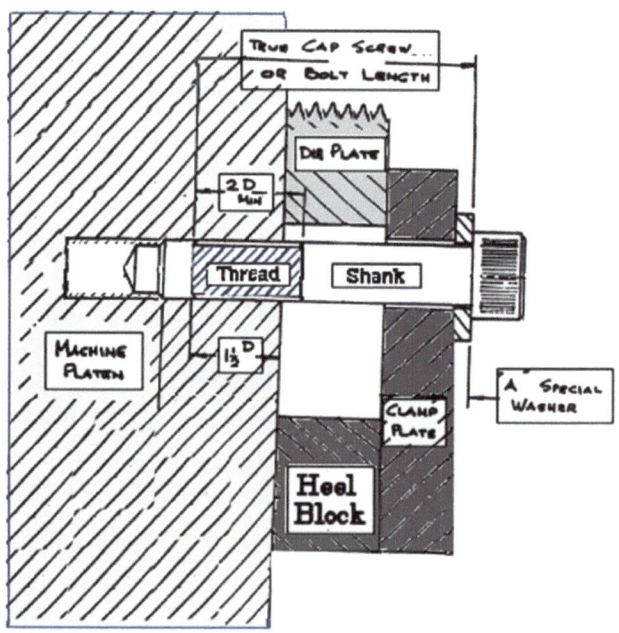

An Introduction to Basic Elements
And Why we use them

When using clamps the heel block of the clamp will be slightly larger than the back plate thickness, if the back plate has been scolloped out to suit a set size clamp then the width of this section of backplate should be slightly smaller than the heel block. The reason for this is that force is required to be exerted onto the tool, not the heel block. The bolt should also be positioned as close to the tool as possible, this will ensure the force is leaning toward the tool. If the heel block is excessive in size, what will happen is (to magnify this issue) say the heel block is twice the size of the back plate, even if the bolt length is ideal and as close to the tool as possible, only the tip of the clamp will be touching the tool and not an even flat surface. This is the difference between holding yourself up by your finger as opposed to using your hand.

When tightening the bolt, don't place the clamp up against the tool block, the reason for this is that as you tighten the bolt the clamp will in turn spread slightly, if you are up against a stop, the majority of the force will be exerted there (against the stop) and not against the back plate where you need it, obviously there will be some force given to the back plate but just back off the clamp position slightly from any stop to allow for expansion.

An Introduction to Basic Elements
And Why we use them

There is a manufactured clamp called the banana clamp which is designed to not require heel blocks.

Don't misconstrue this design clamp and use flat steel clamps in the same manner. The banana clamps are specifically designed with directional positions for the bolt that will exert pressure where it is needed.

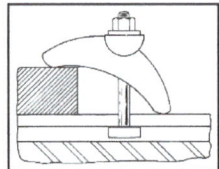

An Introduction to Basic Elements
And Why we use them

...Hang Water Hoses up.

When doing a die change hang up the water hoses and ancillary leads.

Why you may ask...well there are several reasons, consider a tool that has a lot of hoses, you disconnect and throw them on the floor behind you, sooner or later you will trip or stumble on one or more of these hoses, they have now become a safety hazard, YOUR safety and others are at risk and it only takes one hose for an unfortunate accident to occur. What about when you put the next tool in...if you have hung up the hoses, or laid them out on the floor in a safe manner away from your immediate working area, choosing a hose at the optimum length to suit what you need is easy. the longest ones verses the shortest ones, it is now easy to complete the plumbing of the next tool. If however the hoses are just one jumbled mess on the floor, choosing the required length hose becomes a chore, and untangling it from the others makes it a time consuming messy job which is easily side-tracked. This practice will ensure your safety, the safety of others in the workplace, faster die change times, and let's not forget...a messy workplace promotes more mess, a clean workplace promotes the same trains of thought in others. BE A LEADER, do the right thing by yourself and others.

An Introduction to Basic Elements
And Why we use them

For the Troubleshooter

... Record changes in a machine Log Book.

It is normally considered necessary to record adjustments made to the process in a machine log book. This will assist in the long term with getting to the root cause of the issue at hand.

For example. If the 2nd zone heater band failed during a run, the thermocouple would more than likely exhibit an overrun from the heater band before and after this one at fault, thereby during a run you may not get any significant showing on the barrel heats, thereby forcing you to look for alternative causes. Following this train of thought if you were running a job at a lower end of the recommended melt temperature and you lost this heater band, it is feasible that the melt temperature would in fact drop even though it may not be evident on the readouts, this may in turn result in a short shot or stalling of the flow fronts which may (initially) be remedied by increase in the main injection pressure or speed. However, when the machine is turned off at the end of the week and allowed to go cold. On restarting the machine, this heater band will be showing up as not heating and will be replaced, consequently (ideally) the speeds and pressures should be put back to original.

Consider the root cause of the issue discovered.

But if you didn't record your adjustment in a log book attached to the machine, somebody else is now starting the machine, discovering the root cause of an issue, consequently probably (on restart) getting lots of flash or burning and thinking the barrel temps are too hot or the mould is too hot.

An Introduction to Basic Elements
And Why we use them

In the end adjustments are being made that are driving the optimum profiles further and further away from the original settings. Always look for the **Root Cause** of an issue, not just

<u>fix the issue - fix the root cause of the issue</u>.

Sometimes this may not be evident which is why a log book displaying the (at the time) temporary fix should be adhered to and later referred to.

29 OCT 13	21:00	LOADED OP. PROGRAM FOR BEN BARKER BBV	DAN
	22:30	Talked to SRI Host to Host	DAN
		Left op. imp program running after sending a host dead message to imp.	DAN

The format for a Log book should display the date and time, it should show what was adjusted and why, also the person who made the adjustment. This way the person who made the adjustment can be approached and asked what other things were adjusted prior to settling on this latest adjustment. (what doesn't fix the issue gets put back, right!)

An Introduction to Basic Elements
And Why we use them

Do not be afraid to put your name to an adjustment.

I am a firm believer of **Bring everyone up to the same level**, not people finding a fix to a problem and then keeping it to themselves. If an adjustment is made which is put in the book, ultimately doesn't fix the issue and some-one else comes along and finds a more permanent fix, then inform the first person of the fix,, as well as updating the log book. that way not only is everyone on the same page (so to speak) but a better understanding of the process at hand is evidenced. To explain further, say adjustment 1 to a short shot was to increase the tool temperature. That fixed the issue at the time, consequently was entered into the book, however...later (overnight) when the ambient temperature dropped severely, more shorts were evident and simple increases in speed or pressures were giving other issues, finally this 2nd person discovers that the head element on the barrel had gone, and although was allowing material to flow was resulting in a premature cold front stalling and not quite making the fill as easy as it should. So...in conclusion the 1st adjuster wasn't (one upped) by the 2nd adjuster, the 1st one found a fix that seemed to be the root cause, however (as is always the case) sooner or later the root cause will show itself that doesn't make the 2nd adjuster any better or worse than the 1st adjuster, it is simply a sequence of events which is why the log book should ALWAYS be completed.

Dankerr Enterprises

An Introduction to Basic Elements
And Why we use them

Conversely... Let's say the 2nd adjuster found the root cause of the issue (head heater band), replaced it and kept the fix to himself. Firstly every time this issue returns then this 2nd adjuster consistently gets approached to fix the issue (possibly this heater element fix is not a good comparison to a fix, but hopefully you are getting the gist of what I am saying). Now what happens when that 2nd adjuster is away and the issue rears it's head again? What happens is management will see that a machine is either running with a very high reject rate (not good) or is down (off) until this 2nd adjuster is back at work. (also not good) In my opinion this is a sackable offence.

Ease the frustration of all around you and share the load.. Sooner or later this ultimate fix will be found by some-one else, and if he does the right thing and shares the load by entering into the log book he will get lots of accollades from management and peers alike, and this 2nd adjuster who kept the fix to himself is left out in the cold. Can you see by what I am saying, this Log Book is a Friend to yourself, others in the same position AND management. they see Leadership by way of entries and showing -everyone- the way forward.

Share the Load

An Introduction to Basic Elements
And Why we use them

...Change ONE thing at a time.

It is essential that when an adjustment is made, if it doesn't fix the problem at hand, then put it back and try something else. You will find throughout any/all of your training through plastics, from whatever source, this will be drummed into you

This will help explain in depth WHY.

When trying to fix a part burning issue by (say) dropping the barrel temps, dropping the back pressure and lowering the injection speed all at once, All three of these adjustments may fix the issue at hand but what one did? If you then start getting shorts, what adjustment do you put back? see what I mean? After this flurry of adjustments possibly leaving you with other issues, the root fix for this may be a cleaning of the vents in the tool, but you will never know because you are now chasing a different series of problems. Therefore not only have you adjusted things that didn't need adjusting, but when some-one else comes along (on shift changeover for example) how do they then get back to original settings in order to further pursue a more permanent and lasting fix if what has just been adjusted has not fixed the issue or typically made things a whole lot worse.

Change one thing at a time, if it doesn't fix the problem, put it back and try something else.

An Introduction to Basic Elements
And Why we use them

Another explanation for doing this would be, What if you dropped the barrel temps but started getting shorts so increased the back pressure, this would place the barrel temps lower than a previously set optimum but by increasing the back pressure you will be increasing the melt temperature back up to where it was in the first place, consequently not fixing the issue at hand, but putting the settings possibly at a lower limit giving no leeway to further adjustments.

Once a job is running and running well, there are things that will throw the mouldings out such as ambient temperature, hot water unit dropping out, barrel heater band not heating or losing a leg. These are just a couple of the myriad of reasons why a slight adjustment may need to be made to an already proven process, which is why when an adjustment needs to be made, it should be one adjustment at a time, which will (in turn) guide you to the root cause of the issue or the long lasting fix.

An Introduction to Basic Elements
And Why we use them

...Typical 1st Adjustment

For me I typically try an excessive adjustment to prove whether or not this will fix my issue, if it does, then I proceed to fine tune the adjustment before making a record of the fix put in place on the machines log book. Sometimes however a major adjustment to (for example) injection speeds may not be feasible on some moulds, your own gut feel or judgment is required in these cases.

Typically you will find yourself in situations where you are confronted with an old mould which has run many, many times before and you know it's characteristics, in which case when you go for an injection speed adjustment to see if it will fix your issue at hand you will typically know how far to go to test the fix. To explain this further, if the profile has a slow injection speed, increase the speed to say medium system speed, this will highlight a fix for the issue at hand or not, allowing you to then fine tune or put back and try something else.

I have found it (over time) quite frustrating changing only 1 or 2 percent at a time, not quite sure whether or not the issue at hand is easing, consequently I have either gone away from this and tried something else, only to come back later on and try a larger adjustment, wasting time, effort, causing rejects and frustration.

An Introduction to Basic Elements
And Why we use them

... Finding the Optimum Gate Freeze Time.

Sometimes you will get variances that are not stable, even when making adjustments they don't hold firm leading you to the thought that "I wonder if the gates are frozen" As you will know, the process of filling a mould is injecting to changeover at 9/10ths of the fill then changing over to hold pressure to just push the flow fronts forward enough to fill the part and hold that position until the gates freeze off. At this point (gate freeze) you are assured no material will flow back through the gates leaving you with possible sinks or short shots.

The process of assuring the time of gate freeze is to take all time off of the hold time. weigh the part or parts, all cavities including the sprue. Now add one second at a time, weighing the parts as you go. you will go through a stage of the weight increasing until it gets to the point of no change in weight from the previous shot. You will know at this point the gates are frozen and no material will return back through the gate. Typically you will add one further second to the hold time in order to assure gate freeze. During this process, it is recognised that this is a previously optimised process given that the speeds, positions and pressures have been previously optimised and set. For further instructions and 'how to' suggestions on die trialing, refer to "the meat and potatoes of Plastic Injection Moulding" "Explaining the Why in die trialing"

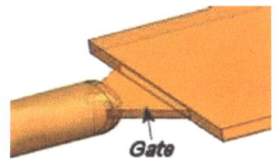

Gate

An Introduction to Basic Elements
And Why we use them

...Finding the Optimum Melt Temperature

Over the years I have come across setups that include some barrel temperatures that have been (let's say) controversial. With that in mind I think it's pertinent to include in this first book a description of what the barrel temperature profile should look like.

Firstly, the profile of the barrel should be coolest at the rear (throat end) and hottest at the front. Some other factors enter into the equation here. The material manufacturers issue recommendations for their materials which give an ideal profile, but typically this profile is for a standard screw and no mixing head incorporated in the screw. There are different screw types you can get which needs to be factored into their recommended profile. For example, a high compression screw (middle zones) would be sheering the material more in these zones and consequently giving a higher melt temperature than suggested. Also if there is a mixing head included in the design of the screw, this gives the material a torturous path to pass through, which (as the design dictates) will mix the material before leaving the barrel. This is typically to mix master batches with the base material. If a nozzle with a mixing insert, inserted into the rear of the nozzle is used, this is also a method of blending materials but would also sheer the materials on exit. Okay, what does all this mean. I would recommend that whenever trying a new material or setting some parameters for the barrel temperatures that you take the manufacturers recommendations with a pinch of salt. This is not to say they are wrong, but there are so many other parameters that come into play. At the end of the day you definately need to adhere to their recommended melt temperature.

An Introduction to Basic Elements
And Why we use them

This is the temperature of the material on exiting the nozzle. As I said earlier I have come across some wonderful settings over the years which have a profile of (something along these lines) 220c at the rear, then 225c, 260c, 235c at the nozzle. (I picked on a small profile for impact.) I would suggest that the melt temperature in this instance would probably be in the region of around 250c even given the nozzle of 235c, there would be override of temperature on the melt. At this juncture you need to remember that the nozzle temperature should be set as the controlling temperature prior to entering the mould. If a hot runner is incorporated into the tool then this should be set as an extension of the nozzle with the controlling points being the gate or tips. The material profile should be from the rear to the head, this should make and maintain the recommended melt temperature, leaving the nozzle to control the flow, (as in drool, freeze off etc). Now the reason why the above profile would be incorrect is this. The heater elements attached to the barrel would be doing overtime trying to understand what you are asking of them. With the zone registering 260c, either side of that element would be showing overrun, where the 225c zone would be trying to cool or not draw a current whereas the 260c element is trying to (because of the profile) heat the whole section of the barrel in this area on it's own. Don't forget this element is trying to maintain 260c, the previous element is trying to maintain 225c, if the 260c zone is achieving it's end, then given the override this previous zone would be (basically) switched off most of the time, if not all the time. This practice at the end of the day results in lots of burnt out heater elements.

need to adhere to their recommended melt temperature.

An Introduction to Basic Elements
And Why we use them

The profile should be coolest at the rear slowly building to the head which (at this point) should have achieved the recommended melt temperature given by the manufacturer, leaving the nozzle to control the melt prior to entering the mould.

In the early days nylons used to have a reverse profile where the requirement was to melt the material in the barrel early, then drop off slowly toward the head in order to control this type of material, we used to use reverse tapered nozzles as well, but these days the manufacturers have stabilised the majority of materials even to the extent of additives that would blow your mind. For example stainless steel with abs, I kid you not.

The majority of the time, if you stick to these basic principles, your machine and melt temperature will stay stable allowing you to follow up with the ideal flow into the mould.

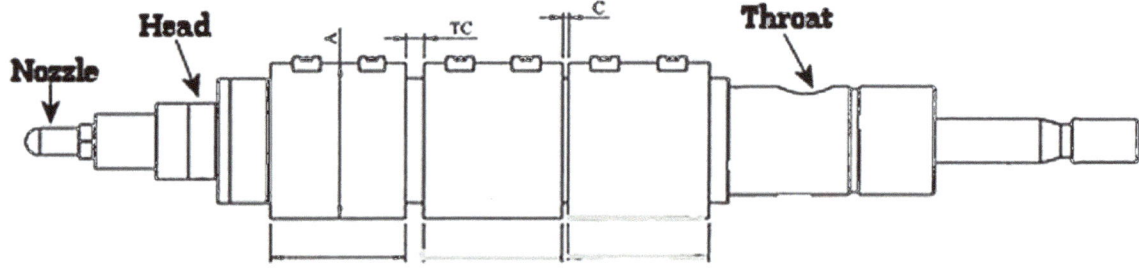

An Introduction to Basic Elements
And Why we use them

... Erratic Cushion

There are times when the screw keeps bottoming out (injecting all the way forward) which is not the ideal. The reason for confirming a cushion is to ensure consistency in the filling of the mould. With some material left in front of the screw at the full forward position, some leeway is acceptable because you will still get a consistent pack, but if the screw bottoms out then this consistency is lost.

At this point it is very easy to say the screw and/or check ring is worn. Which is where material slips back over the flights of the screw or past the check ring allowing the screw to travel forward without pushing material in front of it. But there are some things you need to understand before making that judgement. Take for example, a foreign object or higher melt granule getting lodged in behind the check ring and it's seat, this would not allow a seating of the ring and hence material would bypass the ring and allow the screw to move forward without forcing material in front of it. Sometimes a simple purge with a purging agent is all that is needed, other times a raise in barrel temps then a heavy purge is required. Knowledge of the previous job and materials will help make the decision in this instance. Sometimes by forcing a definitive clearance between the check ring and it's seat by increasing an initial fast injection speed at the beginning accompanied by a rather large suck back at the end of the fill can force the check ring to do it's job.

An Introduction to Basic Elements
And Why we use them

One of the biggest things I look for when trying to combat this type of erratic or no cushion situation is by watching the screw move forward, if it makes changeover and holds for a period of time (possibly 1 or 2 seconds) then slowly moves forward to bottom out, the chances are high that either the check ring is not seating as explained above, or indeed the check ring or smear head is worn. This holding pressure for a second or two is indicating that material is being forced in front of the screw to the point of pack but is not able to hold that position showing a bleed back. Typically if there is a foreign body or higher melt granule inhibiting the seating of the check ring, you won't get that initial holding for a period of time, the screw will stall at changeover and keep moving forward which is purely the hydraulics and moog valve coming into play not the physical seating of the check ring. As a temporary measure if purging as indicated above doesn't help, may be to reduce the pack pressures to ensure a hold pattern. It is possible that the design of the tool may not allow this to occur but if some leeway is allowed, try reducing the pack so that the screw is held in that forward position without bottoming out, until the gate is frozen.

An Introduction to Basic Elements
And Why we use them

Okay...

I hope this has helped guide or re-kindle some basic elements. Let's face it, it is so easy to get blase' about a job when you are doing it day in and day out, but it is also just as easy to do things the right way, saving yourself time, energy and let's also not forget 'being seen' to be doing the right thing by the Boss.

Keep an eye out for some in-depth troubleshooting guides and, more in-depth Diesetting Guides.

Happy - Plastics Injection Moulding.

Danny Kerridge

An Introduction to Basic Elements
And Why we use them

About the Author

Just a quick Foreword about myself and Experiences.

I have worked in plastics since August of 1984. Recently Retired.

Covered all aspects of the Industry from Operating and 'what the operators have to put up with' through material handling prior to computers and calculators, which for some of you 'old salts' included the use and mix of dry powders as colouring. On to Die setting, which (for information) was where I felt the most comfortable. The reason for this is that I found when you put a tool into the machine from scratch, set it up run and troubleshot initial parameters you get to know how that tool ticks. As opposed to being a Technician and walking behind the Diesetters correcting any faults. Yes it is true, with the knowledge already onboard by the Techs it doesn't take long to come to grips with the tool, I just found it more appealing to start on the front line and be a part of fixing issues at the ground level.

Moving on...I spent a lot of time in the Technicians role including senior technician for a number of years, as a Team Leader (supervisor) position. This position left me training and guiding technicians and diesetters more than dealing with the every day activities on the floor. For those in this position, there is always pressure to get "the hardest" jobs in and running, it always seems to be these jobs where guidance was required, which is where I came into my own. I have worked with multitudes of machines, multitudes of materials and experienced many different workplaces. I hope the following guides assist those requiring a little extra explanation.